# Fall of the Multiverse

# Fall of the Multiverse

Samuli Aalto

Kustantaja: Books on Demand GmbH, Helsinki, Suomi
Valmistaja: Books on Demand GmbH, Norderstedt, Saksa

ISBN: 978-952-498-687-8

# Contents

# Chapter 1

In our multiverse was terrible life, because some of the entities of the multiverse were perfectly wrongful. Other entities of the multiverse weren't just either, but they were living entities. Living entities weren't like other entities, which were appliance enchanted at their best. Other appliance enchanted lived with living appliances and others with destroyed appliances. The more wrongful entities aren't appliance enchanted at all, but they are destroyed from their appliances. All appliance enchanted are worse than living entities, because the living entities are perfectly wrongful entities, who won't die into almost anything.

All our appliance enchanted are in the Creator's system more wrongful than was even imagined. All wrongful entities have been destroyed in modern times due to their injustice, when all wrongful were destroyed. All wrongful are very wrongful still, but there are unbroken appliances over 50 percent in them, when they didn't become destroyed. All the most wrongful are appliance enchanted today, when the world met final judgment. In our final judgment, all the wrongful were destroyed with the help from the spiritual world in the year 2009. In the year 2010, all the rest from the entities to become destroyed went to the dimension of the spiritual world to become destroyed, and from this, no trace was noticed in the physical world or in the spiritual world. All took place on the level of the channels, when the spiritual channels were destroyed with the intimidations and curses of the dying. Either from this one didn't notice any trace in the physical world or in the spiritual world. The Creator knows everything from this, because he is the most channeling entity in our complete universe. Channeling entities know the most about matters, when all entities, which channel, are more intelligent than other humans.

Humans which do not channel are channeling to a lesser extent, because channeling is more cursing than was even imagined. On our channel, there are lots of new creatures, which don't know what to do on our channel. Channeling entities are more cursing than other entities, because on our channels one doesn't allow even anything perfectly wrongful. Channeling entities know from matters more than non-

channeling humans. On our channels, there is
the very wrongful folk, who destroy entities on
the level of the physical world. All our channeling entities are more wrongful than non-
channeling entities, but the ones who channel
are fools even more than others in addition to
all. On our channels, one doesn't allow another
meaning for the non-channeling. On our channels all are wrongful, because the world is
wrongful. All injustice is due to our lacks. All
our injustice is caused by the Creator beginning
from earlier times with his lacking actions. All
writings are wrongful, because lacking writings
are all writings, and lack has to be accepted
from all our writings. All writings are wrongful,
even if they were as perfect as they could. All
lack is due to Creator's deeds from earlier
times.

In the Creator's systems, there are all kinds of
entities.  All entities don't live on planet Earth,
but they live on exoplanets. Our exoplanets are
very wrongful planetoids, where there is a very
wrongful folk. All our exoplanets are more
wrongful than was even imagined. All Creator's systems end to this day, if one wasn't allowed to say anything about exoplanets. All our

exoplanetoids are also constructed from the inside, when the Creator organized on to our exoplanets areas constructed to the inside, because planetoids are planets constructed from their inside. Our planetoid the planet Earth is also constructed from the inside. The scientists won't believe this. However, when such areas constructed to the inside of the planet are matters of faith. Everything functions as channel information the best, however, because channel information is information accepted by the spiritual world. In the spiritual world, there are wrongful spirit entities, which cause false information into the world. All false information is wrongful. Injustice on our channels is quite great from the part of our information, but injustice is more minimal on the spiritual channels than what it is in the real world. In the real world, the devotees of the secret societies and the humans of the system suppress information, when the suppressed information comes forth worse. The suppressed information is important information, but they aren't perfect information, because the Creator has even more perfect information than what the suppressing quarters have. This information is given birth by channeling, when all information is direct information of the spiritual world.

All Creator's information is information given birth by the Creator, which are considered with the help from reasoning ability. The reasoning ability is extremely important to the Creator. Concluded information is such, where the Creator doesn't say anything about matters to other humans, but he learns knowledge from other humans. This knowledge he can use wrongfully by taking advantage or by using it righteously according to his own desires. According to his own desires, the Creator is a wrongful entity. From him one ought to require justice, or otherwise he is wrongful. Wrongfulness in him has developed with time, when he wasn't so wrongful in earlier times as what he is in modern times. In earlier times the Creator was more super enchanted that is worse and along with it, a more wrongful entity still.

Injustices of the Creator were multiple-leveled, when the Creator didn't write anything wrongful in earlier times, although he did write all kinds of writings. All writings like these have remained to modern times as well, but from those haven't survived for modern times other

10

than the most significant works. Such are very many known writings of earlier times. Writings were in earlier times a bit worse than today, when compared even with the Creator's today's writings the less wrongful writings were very popular.

The Creator is a super entity, who doesn't have anything to lose, because he does everything badly. At times, he changes the systems on the level of the spiritual world, when he can end the agreements on the level of the spiritual world anytime. The agreements to the Creator end like so that he checks out such, who have done injustice too much and can't repair their matters. The Creator's appliance has destructive armed forces in his use always. The Creator's appliance does tours with a spaceship as an entity enchanted by his appliance. The Creator does tours with a spaceship also, but he is then more wrongful than the Creator's appliance in the opinion of the spiritual world, because the spiritual world becomes often envious of the Creator's tours with the spaceship. The Creator's tours with a spaceship are spaceship tours enchanted by an appliance, when in the spaceship, there is all possible equipment included. All

possible equipment belongs to the Creator's
actions, when the Creator is distinguished from
others due to his equipment. The spaceship
tours end at times badly, because the Creator is
at times too low-minded on his spaceship tours.
All spaceship tours are bewitched by the Creator, when the spaceships are safer than what
their pilots can uphold. The spaceships are created by the Creator, when the Creator can fly
with the spaceship the best. With a spaceship,
one can fly all around the universe, when in the
universe, there are many spaceships. With the
spaceships one flies a lot to planet Earth as
well.

On our planet Earth, there are many spaceships,
with which one flies by the extraterrestrial entities in the missions of the spaceship policemen.
Our spaceship policemen are the most wrongful
entities on our planet Earth. Planet Earth's
spaceship policemen are changed valars. The
persons in the valars' spaceships are human
looking extraterrestrial beings, who have beau-
tiful facial features. They are pale from their
skin color. The extraterrestrial entities from
outer space are more wrongful than any inhab-
itant of planet Earth. The inhabitants of planet

Earth are more wrongful to the extraterrestrial entities of outer space than what they are towards the inhabitants of planet Earth. In addition, the Creator lives on planet Earth and is also wrongful towards the extraterrestrial entities of outer space. The extraterrestrial entities of outer space are although the most wrongful entities, so the inhabitants of planet Earth have targeted their injustice more towards the extraterrestrial entities of outer space than what the extraterrestrial entities of outer space have targeted the inhabitants of planet Earth.

The Creator is a super entity, which there isn't but one and only entity. Such entities can't be born but otherwise. All the Creator's systems are made by the Creator beginning from earlier times. The Creator's systems are very multiple-leveled, when in the Creator's systems; there is very multiple-leveled activity. Activity is multiple-leveled, as long as all the entities are leveled onto their own levels. Multiple-leveled activity is the best activity of the Creator, when the Creator accepts all his wrongful entities as well, although he would himself be in good set. Entities in good set are usually better than others, because they aren't in good set other than with the help from the Creator's systems. The ones in good set are less wrongful to entities, which the Creator accepts. The Creator accepts everything, but personal acceptance isn't always possible from the Creator either, because he has to develop the universe as well. All the problems of the universe are possible to become solved with the help from the Creator, because the Creator could do everything perfectly.

A perfect entity is an entity created by the Creator, although it isn't, because there are numerous imperfect makings of the Creator. The Creator functions at times with wrongful information wrongfully, when perfectness can't be achieved. Although perfectness is impossible to accomplish, because development violates perfectness, so the need to develop to become better violates perfectness. Perfectness is violated in the end by injustice, which there is in the Creator's systems quite a lot, so that there would be lots of development as well. All wrongful things are placed by themselves in entities already once the entity is born. All our entities are very wrongful, but entities don't still accept their injustice, when injustices continue towards perfectness as long as the Creator controls them.

The Creator's magics are quite straining for humans, because they aren't understood as magic of humans but as magic of some super entity, which everyone knows with some magic. Some magics are on the level of a cursed Creator, when all magics are cursed magics. All cursed magics are magics cursed by the Creator. Magics cursed by the Creator are magics that spoil, when the Creator himself goes along into the cursing activity to create different kinds of experiences and entities. Entities are on the level of the Creator when they dare to become wrongful and go along into the cursing activity due to others. Due to others, the magics cursed by the Creator are very wrongful after getting into wrong hands.

Creator's magics did lots of injustice in earlier times, because the Creator was at times wrongful. Thus, the Creator could become cursed in a terrible way. The Creator's curses were on a very high level. The Creator himself didn't want to become cursed, but when other humans demanded him to become cursed, he most often fulfilled their wish. Wishes from humans led the Creator to become wrongful as a super entity, when the Creator doesn't become cursed, but others become cursed. Curses of others were due to the Creator's systems, when the Creator smiled at the human entities, who were becoming cursed. The Creator's injustices were due to that all suffered due to bad activity, so everyone wanted also the Creator to suffer from his own systems, because they were themselves suffering. All humans who had suffered didn't know how to act in the right way, because they started to cause additional sufferings to humans, when they were marked as the ones to become doomed in later times. The Creator's humans which had suffered received eases to their life in later times, when again those who had caused suffering to others had to be destroyed at the final judgment. All the Creator's entities which suffered are still alive, so the Creator is still as an active entity on our planet Earth. On our planet Earth, there is very much ignorance from this judgment, which met the humanity in our modern times.

Wrongful information is high level magic, with which the Creator functions in our universe. In our universe, the Creator has very much to do, because the Creator is a very high level entity of the world and an entity of the spiritual world as well. The Creator's systems are very high level magics, where there is injustice less than was even imagined. The Creator's systems are very high-quality magics, where the systems of planet Earth are a part of. All Creator's systems are very high-quality systems, which are rotated also in the spiritual world. The systems of the spiritual world are very vast in size in our universe, because it is a system of earlier times, so the Creator has lived on planet Earth the whole time beginning from earlier times, when planet Earth is the planet of the Creator. On the Creator's planet, there is very high level activity, when the Creator modifies the systems of planet Earth for later times.

The Creator has lots of helper spirits, which are for the Creator very important helpers of the Creator. Helpers are very important, because the Creator was hated in earlier times, so the Creator is as cursed helped by the helper spirits. All helper spirits have been destroyed in later times, when the helper spirits have been destroyed to become living entities. The Creator didn't like emotions of the helper spirits in earlier times, but in modern times the helper spirits' emotions are less cursed. In modern times the helper spirits were dying entities, because the Creator gave the helper spirits punishments in modern times. Earlier he only listened to the curses of the helper spirit. The helper spirits destroyed the Creator usually, because the helper spirits were cursed, but the Creator trusted in them with his perfect love. Perfect love is Creator's untruthful activity, when the Creator doesn't do any perfect activity, but he only accepts all faults from his entities. Usually entities are in the opinion of the Creator more wrongful than was even imagined. All wrongful entities are more wrongful than was even imagined, because the Creator is more wrongful than was even imagined.

The Creator is as a super entity very wrongful. Super entities are very wrongful at times. Super entities have age more than other entities, because super entities have survived as living entities beginning from earlier times in our world. Furthermore, super entities are more wrongful than was even imagined. All our super entities are loved by the Creator, because the Creator wouldn't want super entities to die.

18

Our super entities have lots of similarities with each other, but super entities are also opposite to each other. Our super entities have lots of equivalences with the Creator, when our super entities are more wrongful than was even imagined. All our wrongful entities are makings of the super entities. Makings are against our super entities. Makings are hateful towards super entities, because in the Creator's system, makings want to cause damage to our super entities. Our super entities are very wrongful, when the makings are let to punish our super entities.

Our super entities are the most wrongful, when the Creator has given them permission to go wrongful. The permission is given with the help from the system. So that the system would hold up, the system has to give permissions to more developed entities, so that developed entities would develop onto a new level. On the new level, the more developed entities can satisfy themselves better even as appliance enchanted. Appliance enchantments are appliances of the spiritual world accepted by the Creator, which are more wrongful than was even imagined. The appliances of the spiritual world have lots to do with thinking. The auxiliary equipment of the spiritual world that is helping thinking is called appliance enchantment. All our appliance enchantments are at times a bit more wrongful than entities equipped with true functions. Entities are more wrongful than was even imagined. With the help from systems, entities can change to become top wrongful. Injustices are given birth from the deceased parts of the thinking functions, which harm entities themselves, when the entity becomes wrongful to other entities.

The Creator is from the super entities the most super entity like, when the Creator becomes wrongful always at times more temporarily than was even imagined. All wrongful entities are developed by the Creator to create problems, which the Creator should solve by developing his system to last entities, which are more wrongful than others. All more wrongful entities have been destroyed with the final judgment in modern times. All the most wrongful entities were destroyed in the first half of the 21st century, because there was a more disadvantage than advantage from them. Wrongful entities are in the Creator's system the ones who cause problems, which had to be destroyed in later times. Thus, the universe develops by learning new matters from the entities which do injustice. Wrongful were destroyed due to that too plentiful injustice destroyed the complete going on into completely obsolete. When entities were too wrongful, too many problems came into the world, when injustices didn't grow in accordance with development, but injustices went out of control. The spiritual world was also functioning wrongfully like this. All the entities of the spiritual world were very sad due to the destruction, but also this was wrongful, because they grieved only due to the decrease in destructive activity.

The Creator's injustices are on a very high level, because the Creator is the most super entity like from the super entities, which is also very far sighted. The Creator sees always some need for advancement in injustice. All injustices are cursed by the Creator already in earlier times. In earlier times the Creator rotated very high level activity. Very high level activity was due to the level of know-how of the Creator, which is higher than what people's level of know-how is usually. All humans are bewitched by the Creator already beginning from earlier times.

All earlier times were bewitched by the Creator,
when the Creator planned monstrous activity,
where there was both good and evil accompanied. All Creator's systems were on a very high
level already in earlier times. In modern times
the systems are functioning with the help from
the system of sanctity even on a higher level
than what they have been even in earlier times.
In earlier times with the help from the victim
system, the Creator didn't do any good things,
but he did wrongful things, so that all would
develop faster to become just activity.

All activity is on a very high level while made
in accordance with the Creator's system, so the
Creator functions usually in accordance with
the system. Furthermore, other super entities,
which have more meanings than what many
other entities have, function in accordance with
the Creator's system. The Creator seeks continuously better functioning for himself and for his
system, which is a system that is held up by the
spiritual world. The system held up by the spiritual world is the highest system of all, which is
held up by the entities of the spiritual world and
entities of the world. All wrongful matters are
wrongful in very many ways, so injustice

should be avoided, but not to be afraid of. Avoiding injustice doesn't prevent injustice, but injustices become minimal by avoiding them, which is the best functionality when thought farsightedly. Farsighted thoughts are the best thoughts, when far sight is a virtue among others. Farsighted thoughts do well for humans; as long as far sight is on the level of the Creator. The gift of far sight is a great benefit for the functions of an entity, because so one avoids greater problems, which are due to short-sighted thinking. The entities of the Creator are very different from each other, so the Creator's entities differ also from their functions from each other. The Creator's entities have a very sacred life, were they wrongful or not, because the most wrongful are guided by the system, so all life is sacred also the wrongdoers'. The Creator's injustices are very far-reaching, when the injustices are very destructive to the functions of the Creator. Action requires injustice, although, when the Creator doesn't care from his acts of injustice.

# Chapter 2

All the Creator's entities are more wrongful than was even imagined in our spiritual world. In the spiritual world, there are very wrongful groups, from which the group of the Multiverse was the worst from all the other humans. In the spiritual world have the most wrongful groups been destroyed. Groups were destroyed in our modern times with the appliance of the final judgment, which took responsibility for the final judgment in accordance with the prophecies. Prophecies were very wrongful, because prophecies have destroyed so many spirit entities of humans, because even wars have been started with prophecies. Prophecies are more wrongful than was even imagined, because with the help from prophecies have also lots of bad been done on behalf of the Creator. The Creator doesn't do evil willingly, but like the most wrongful groups, also the Creator does lots of injustice along with mischief. All evildoers are hated by the Creator. The wrongdoers had consciousness about matters, which was a lot more wrongful than what the Creator had while he was doing injustice.

All our wrongdoers are very alike when compared with the Creator's wrongdoing, but the difference is that the Creator relies on the permission thinking more often than other wrongdoers. Permission thinking is a product of the Creator's imagination, because the Creator has created the systems, with which one gives permissions for wrongdoing. The Creator's imagination is then often also right in relation to how wrongdoing is wrongful. Furthermore, the permission thoughts of others are always wrongful, because injustice shouldn't be done even with the help from permissions.

All treaties end always when the Creator has been wrongful towards other human entities. All Creator's injustices are very difficult, because the Creator is wrongful when he wants to. All experiences of injustice are injustice on the level of the Creator, because the Creator is always aware of his wrongfulness. All wrongdoers are losers after a punishment on the level of the Creator, because the Creator has created agreements with the right minded and not with the wrongdoers. The Creator likes from injustice less than what wrongdoers like from injustice. Wrongful Creator's thoughts are wrongful in the opinion of the spiritual world. Spirit entities which have done injustice are very wrongful often, because spirit entities have lives in an environment, where wrongdoing is more possible than in the world. Wrongdoers are often very cursed entities, because such wrongdoers have done so much injustice, that they can't even find new ways to do injustice. Wrongdoers are very cursed and there is a need to create eases for wrongdoers, with which injustice could be done less. For wrongdoers one so has to create eases, because our wrongdoers are very cursed. Cursed entities are very wrongful, because cursed entities have died spiritually and physically. All Creator's magics are more wrongful than magics of other humans, but the Creator does injustice more with the help from permissions than many other entities.

All the Creator's magics are more wrongful than magics of other humans, because the Creator is as a super entity a very wrongful entity when compared with other wrongful entities. Injustices of other wrongful entities are more minimal than the injustices of the Creator, but the Creator's injustices are part of the Creator's work, which others don't have to do. The Crea-

26

tor has to repair the systems into better condition in almost every life of his. All Creator's injustices are cursed injustices to a lesser extent, because they are clearer injustices than the injustices of other entities. All Creator's injustices are very similar with the injustices of other Creator's injustices, because the Creator acts with core information from matters, when the injustices become simpler. All Creator's injustices have been destroyed with the Multiverse, because the Creator has created the entities of the Multiverse, which knew from the Creator's magic the most. All Creator's magics were well-known for the entities of the Multiverse, because the Creator was more wrongful than was even imagined with the help from the Multiverse. In the Multiverse were more wrongful entities, which felt that they were victim entities, but on the other hand, they caused more victims for themselves than other entities of the spiritual world. This kind of causing of victims is very wrongful, because victim entities are very wrongful when they cause victims for themselves, because then the ones who cause victims, are in addition to all injustice also as if they were less knowing from their own situation. The entities of the Multiverse weren't the

ones who did sacrifices, but they were the cause
of victims, when they were as if they were allowed to revenge other entities their own sufferings by causing other entities similar sufferings.
Then injustices were very wrongful, because
victim entities weren't allowed to cause same
sufferings as what they had experienced according to the Creator's system, because then advancement isn't born into the universe. With
the Creator's magic nothing should be allowed
to revenge, because revenge doesn't either create advancement. Revenge is so wrongful.

All entities are more wrongful than was even
imagined in the spiritual world. In the spiritual
world, there are wrongful entities, which destroy the activities of the spiritual world. In the
world, there are again human entities destroying
the functions of the world. The functions of the
spiritual world are automatized by far, and one
doesn't even get to destroy them in any way.
Thus have all acts of injustice been prevented.
Wrongdoers in the Multiverse were more
wrongful than what was even imagined. In the
Multiverse one did so much injustice also the
head of the world's humans as expenditure.
One has done lots of evil with the help from the

spiritual world the head of the humans as expenditure. These kinds of injustices have been very common, especially in earlier times. In earlier times one talked in the Multiverse that also the planet Earth should be gotten into the worst possible condition.

The groups of the entities of outer space on our planet Earth are very wrongful groups. These groups are more wrongful than was even imagined. All groups of the entities of outer space are more wrongful, because they live with the magic of the Creator, which one can't use on planet Earth. All entities of planet Earth are so more right minded than the entities of outer space. All entities are more wrongful than was even imagined, because entities hide their injustice. All entities of outer space are more wrongful, because they are vast in their works of evil. All vast injustices are real acts of injustice for our groups of outer space. Into these connects activity of the spaceships, which the entities of outer space do a lot. The entities of outer space are very wrongful also, because they have too much armed forces in their use. So they can destroy lots of other entities with their armed forces. Our groups of outer space have armed forces so much, because the Creator has created them lots of armed forces in relation to the amount of armed forces of planet Earth. The entities of outer space are militaristic. They have a militaristic society system. In a militaristic society system threatening with weapons is continual among the citizens. The groups of outer space have good relations with planet Earth, although they want onto planet Earth also forcibly. They are although let to live on to planet Earth with the help from the spiritual world into lives, which are similar to normal lives, if they only want to come onto planet Earth.

The groups of outer space aren't very good for planet Earth. On our planet Earth there have been done injustice to the groups of outer space in earlier times, and the groups of outer space want to revenge on planet Earth. The entities of outer space are very wrongful entities. Wrongful entities are more intelligent partly than less wrongful entities. Less wrongful entities are very wrongful only at times, and they don't detect the growth of intelligence then, but they are better humans. Humans living with less intelligence are better entities than others, which are very wrongful to other humans. Very wrongful entities are so more intelligent than less wrongful entities, but they are due to their wrongfulness, entities, which are living less good lives. Injustices divide into those, who uphold their injustice by doing injustice or who want to develop themselves in such a way.

Wrongdoers are very special at times, because with the Creator's magic the wrongdoers can remain without punishment. Because wrongdoers are very nervous, can other humans punish them more easily than what they can do to others. All wrongdoers are very rare to other humans at times, because wrongdoers learn magics, with which they can achieve strange things. These wrongdoers are quite limited number from humans, because very few humans change to wrongdoers. Wrongdoers are rarely wrongful originally, because wrongdoers have learned injustice on their own. Students of injustice are often more wrongful than others already once the spirit entity is born.

Spirit entities are more wrongful than other entities, because spirit entities are more intelligent entities. The more intelligent entities are always more wrongful than other entities. The injustice of the spirit entities is very wrongful, because our spirit entities have lots of injustice. The injustice of the spirit entities can't be observed by anyone so easily, because they hide their injustice. Injustice is hidden due to the injustice of others, so that other entities wouldn't gain permission for punishment too easily. Our wrongdoers are very wrongful very often, because our wrongdoers are very wrongful full-time. In our world, there are also entities, which are only doing injustice. Our wrongdoers are more wrongful than has even been imagined in the spiritual world. Our wrongdoers have very wrongful thoughts, when our wrongdoers can't do anything else than injustice. All our wrongdoers are completely wrongful entities, who can't do anything else than injustice.

All entities become under punishment while doing injustice. All entities are while doing injustice more wrongful than what was imagined in the spiritual world. All wrongful entities are very wrongful from their own opinion as well. All injustices are very wrongful, because they make development difficult and slow it down while being too vast. Too vast injustices

are very different, so they are at times support-
ed, because they only are different than what
other injustices are. All injustices aren't permitted at all. All injustices are different than other
injustices. Other injustices are dangerous a little
when compared with others. All injustices are
injustice according to the Creator's system.
Behind all the injustices is evil will, which is
given birth by lack of thought. All injustices are
very different, because wrongdoers learn different kinds of injustices. The problem of all injustices is the non-compliance with the Creator's
systems. All the problems which are against the
Creator's system are very diverse.

In the Creator's system, there is lots of high
level injustice. Injustice is on a high level, when
all injustices are forgotten and one does new
injustice like one wouldn't have done any injustice earlier. All injustices are on a high level in
some dimension, so in a dimension; injustices
come about in the worst possible way. The real-
ization of injustices depends on the Creator's
system, in such way, that: do the entities of the
spiritual world want to receive a permission to
accomplish the injustices? All injustices are
very wrongful also in accordance with the Crea-

tor's system. Thus, the Creator has given a possibility to do injustice less than what one could do in accordance with one's own will. Injustice in accordance with one's own will is the most wrongful. All injustices aren't really injustices, but they are mistakes, which should be repaired. All injustices are very cursing, because injustices become cursing when the Creator's systems are in bad condition from the part of the injustices.

All the Creator's systems are very special, because the Creator is very versatile. The Creator's systems are special due to that the Creator has created them with a very special kind of activity. Then the Creator has had to do work during his lives to build his systems. The Creator's systems are holier than other systems usually. All the Creator's systems will work even better in later times, because the Creator builds them continuously.  All the Creator's systems are doing injustice still although, because perfectness can't exist, because into everything always belongs doing injustice. Wrongdoing is very normal activity from humans and from the entities of the spiritual world as well. Without injustice there wouldn't be development, because perfectness is even more wrongful than a single injustice. In perfectness injustice is held as a secret matter, when development isn't being created.

Injustices are able to become overthrown with a system which considers everything. A system that considers everything is still always slightly wrongful, because new things appear always, which the system hasn't yet considered. All systems are also slightly wrongful from their basis, because injustice is within the basis of all systems. Systems have been created as the supporting pillars of development and because development has to exist always, there also has to be always a system. Without systems, life can't exist at all, because without systems, nothing can even cohere. Even the atomic world requires systems so that it could uphold the material world. Upholding the material world was very difficult in earlier times, when the material world was looser. Then one could use magical powers, due to that spirit entities could use special powers with the help from the holes in the system of the material world. The material world is nowadays constructed on the level of the spiritual world, when there are very few holes and then one also can't receive magical powers into one's use. Once the material world has been fully developed, new worlds will become constructed; where is a lot to develop from the part of the system. This work belongs to the Creator, and he also acts continuously doing this work.

# Chapter 3

During personal problem times all went upside down, because the personal problems are very cursing. Personal problems are very cursing, because personal problems make everything impossible finally. Personal problem times were very cursing on planet Earth, like they were at the groups of outer space as well. Personal problem times have begun around 6000 BC cursed by the Creator. Just before the beginning of chronology begun more terrible going on, when the Creator cursed religions onto planet Earth. All the inhabitants of planet Earth have died due to religions at least once. The entire Creator's deals end to this day, if one wasn't allowed to write about the influence of religions on our planet Earth. All the inhabitants of planet Earth are so very religious entities. Entities are religious, when entities have religion in their mind during at least one lifetime in the past 500 years. All latest years have killed the Creator onto the level of a small human. Such has the Creator been earlier as well, that he is only as a small human among us. All the things made by the Creator are very religious, because the Creator is a spirit entity which belongs to the basic members of religions. Spirit entities belong to religion, if the spirit entity has been as a founding member of a religion. Founding members of religions are very different when compared with each other, because with the Creator's agreement can anyone start to be a founding member of religions by being useful to the religion.

Religions are founded systems for the humans of the world, so that they would understand from the functions of the spiritual world, at times, when the spiritual world is more hidden. All the entities of the spiritual world are very similar with the humans of the world. The only difference is in the surroundings, when the spiritual world can do different things than what the humans can do on planet Earth, for example, the groups of outer space are slightly closer to the actions of the spiritual world when compared with planet Earth. The entities of the spiritual world are more wrongful than the inhabitants of planet Earth, because they have fewer systems. The entities of the spiritual world have as their system the permission system, but they are allowed to act very freely, doing also injustice at times. The action of the spiritual world is then more wrongful than what would be allowed on planet Earth. The systems of planet Earth don't allow action done freely, because on planet Earth is the people's ability to act wrongfully been limited, when the inhabitants of planet Earth are better humans with the help from their systems. Such is very promoting, but not as enjoyable as what the action in the spiritual world is. Action is wrongful, if the spiritual world is more wrongful towards the permission system. Such is action doomed to destruction.

It is very wrongful to function with the Creator's agreement with the help from the permission system. The Creator's agreement has already very long tradition beginning from earlier times. All systems have been destroyed in the spiritual world today, with the help from the permission systems. All our permission systems are created by the Creator in our modern times. This isn't true although from the part of all systems. All systems aren't actually created by the Creator in modern times, but the Creator has created systems throughout history, from which some have remained up to modern times from earlier times. All our permission systems are very wrongful due to their lacks. All systems are like living entities, which are rotated by the Creator, angels, demons and dimensional entities. All systems are very wrongful on our planet Earth, because on planet Earth, there is a very wrongful folk, which holds good still today as well. All wrongful entities are both good and bad entities, because injustice is handled in a different category. Wrongfulness is so perfectness decreasing, but this again isn't wrongful, because in a matter of fact, perfectness is unjust. In perfectness injustice is blossoming, because even the Creator's deals end in a too perfect atmosphere. All atmospheres are wrongful finally, because the atmospheres don't ever fulfill all criteria. The criteria are strict to advance the wrongful system. The operators of the wrongful system are very cursed, because while doing injustice entities become cursed even more permanently. Thus, injustice is blossoming among the operators of the system. All wrongful are destroyers of the Creator's system. The Creator's systems are very wrongful, because the Creator is very wrongful often. This is due to that injustices shouldn't be allowed to end up supporting other humans, because they will become destroyed easier than the Creator both spiritually and physically. All injustices are wrongful even when made with the Creator's agreement.

The Creator's deals have ended today, when the Creator achieved to build a new system to prevent the giving of wrongful permissions. Wrongful permissions were as a pain for everyone in our modern times. The entire Creator's systems end to this kind of permission giving, where one asks for killing permission to some entities. These kinds of permissions were used in earlier times. Earlier times were very wrongful, because killing permissions were given so much, that at times one fought continually wars for injustice. Our wrongful warriors were very serious wrongdoers, because there was vanity with in their actions. Action was so wrongful, because the Creator wanted to see warrior action quite a lot. Nowadays, wars are fought to a lesser extent than in earlier times, because the Creator's systems are developed in modern times to oppose war action.

Creator's warriors were very wrongful also in earlier times. The warriors did their evil work to advance the universe. The universe developed

very slowly, because the universe has a consciousness, which is slow from its intelligence.
Other consciousnesses are slower from their
intelligence, because slow intelligence produces
wrongful entities. Everything functions in the
most wrongful way. Usually slow intelligence
is better than intelligence functioning with fast
speed. Intelligence is very wrongful when used
wrong. Incorrectly used injustices are injustices
in accordance with the Creator's system. The
Creator's systems were very wrongful in earlier
times, because the Creator did so much injustice. All injustices were Creator's injustices
originally, when the Creator did things to add
more wrongfulness. To add more wrongfulness
the Creator made plans of war for all the
wrongful especially. To add more wrongfulness
the Creator made lots of war plans especially
for his occult meaningful entities. All Creator's
injustices were on the level of war plans, because the Creator's injustices were even more
wrongful than the war plans. The Creator's
injustice was killing magic for Creator's own
systems, when the Creator destroyed himself
into more wrongful than we can even imagine.
The Creator destroyed himself into a wrongful
entity, so that the systems would develop faster.

The Creator has enchanted our faster systems already in earlier times into faster than human intelligence. The Creator's intelligence was very different in earlier times than in modern times.

In modern times all injustice was vaster on the spiritual level and on the physical level in the end times. Then there were wars as well, where many humans died. In good emotions they weren't, because they were taught too much wrongful magic in earlier times. All wrongful magic was on the level of personal problem magic, with which humans were made miserable. Humans were very wrongful, because personal problems grew to become very great in the minds of humans. All wrongful problems are very wrongful when caused to others. All magic is so very different when accomplished in different times. All injustice is accomplished in every way in some dimension, because otherwise it wouldn't be learned to repair, because injustice is self-destructive even without the Creator's system. All systems end to this, if wrongfulness were more destructive than fairness, with which one overcomes wrongfulness.

Injustice is very vast in the more wrongful Creator's system. In the wrongful system, there are destroyed entities as virtual mirrored entities, which have good occult meaning. Occult meaning is in good entities the origin of all wrongfulness. All injustice is on the level of antichrist in our today. Today the occult meaning vanished from planet Earth in the opinion of the entities of outer space. In their opinion, all are wrongfully perfect on the level of the entities of outer space, and then one doesn't need the Creator's systems on the planet. All Creator's magics are about to disappear from planet Earth in modern times. In modern times the Creator's activity has been worse for the entities of outer space, because he has cared from planet Earth too much. All excessive things are very wrongful, when the Creator destroyed himself due to planet Earth. Due to planet Earth destroying oneself has taken place by doing injustice. By doing injustice, he destroyed himself on the level of the physical world into bad physical condition, when he couldn't do almost any true things physically. Physical appearance is frail in him. Because he is as a super entity helped by helper spirits, is he a super entity still. He channels lots of things, also writings. The

44

origin of all writings is the Creator also, because the spiritual world helps writers and the spiritual world is created by the Creator.

Writings created by the Creator are very wrongful at times for humans, because he doesn't care from revealing of wrongfulness in himself. All injustice is created by the Creator, so injustices become very high level. Injustices come forth after the most problematic matters, when the problems are started to be solved. Then wrongdoers try to prevent the solving of the problem, because the wrongdoer doesn't want to become revealed as the cause of problems. Our wrongdoers have lots of plans on a high level to avenge all our systems. Our systems are very wrongful for wrongdoers, so they have to be stronger than other humans. Strengths come from sacrificing mood, so the Creator has destroyed them perfectly into grouch entities. Entities are at times more wrongful than we can even imagine, that is why entities have to be destroyed still on this day. The Creator has bewitched everything to add injustice. Wrongful thoughts are adding injustice the most. All injustices are enchanted by the Creator, when one should take injustices seriously, because wrongdoers take otherwise too lightly, if they weren't forced to become serious.

All injustices are created by the Creator already in earlier times, because the Creator cries from laughter to all entities, which possess perfect functioning. Perfect functioning is wrongful, because then one limits the development function. Development function is a very right minded procedure, with which development can be carried out. If the development function is limited, one imagines that in finalized situation, everything is perfect, but this is impossibility due to limited functioning. Limited functions have been labeled also as wrongful, although, in reality, limiting is wrongful. Limiting is wrongful, because limitations are restricting true functions. With the help from the true functions development is being created, when wrongful functioning is limited to its minimum. Bordered functions are limited very wrongfully. Limited are also advancing things at times. Then is also a wrongful system born, which has been created only to destroy entities. Like this, can also take place at times, because the spirit entities are rather wrongful than righteous.

Only the Creator is more righteous than other
entities. He holds up righteousness in other
humans with his system from the spiritual
world. Entities can be maintained with the help
from the system for a very long time, although
they were themselves wrongful. As wrongful,
entities become destroyed finally, if injustice
continues endlessly without a change. Even
destroyed entities can be held up with appliance
enchantments. Then the destroyed entities
aren't comparable with living entities, but they
are spiritually robots. All our robots are helped
by the spiritual world throughout their lives, if
they don't break their original appliance enchantments, because the spiritual world has
promised them support in accordance with the
appliance enchantments to uphold the appliance
enchantments. With the help from appliance
enchantments, one can do work of the spiritual
world in the world for example. All the entities
of the spiritual world are partly appliance enchanted, but the Creator is appliance enchanted
the least. He has also at times dead appliances.
Functions are better as appliance enchanted
than as dead. Appliance enchantments are
breakable in an eased way, by breaking inten-
tionally the appliances of the spiritual world.

The appliances of the spiritual world are very strange to think about, but they are simpler than we can even imagine. They are only automatized thoughts. Thoughts are automatized, if the appliance enchantments are unbroken. Otherwise the thoughts of the dead are in death magic in accordance with the broken parts, and the living parts function with the Creator's magic.

All who are dead from their spirit have died already in earlier times. All who are appliance enchanted have had to accept the Creator's deals for constructing the appliance enchantments. Constructing can take place anywhere, because appliance enchantments can be built anywhere. The appliance enchantments are usually unbroken for the dead from their spirit, especially in modern times. In modern times the dead from their spirit didn't receive a possibility to break the appliance enchantments with wrongful activity, because the spirit entities were limited from their functions. All appliance enchanted humans are at times difficult with the help from their appliance enchantments, because the appliance enchantments aren't comparable with the living parts of the spirit, with which one becomes angry almost never. Furthermore, the ones dead from their spirit and who have the appliance enchantments broken don't easily become angry. The ones who are appliance enchanted have an eased position, in which the appliance enchanted do injustice with their own permission limited by the appliance enchantments. The ones who are appliance enchanted do their evil work, when the appliance enchanted kill spiritually other appliance enchanted. Other appliance enchanted are although more wrongful in such a situation, because the appliance enchanted comment humans more easily than the dead from their spirit or living.

With appliance enchantments commenting is eased, because the appliance enchantments tell wrongful information. With the help from appliance enchantments commenting does bad result to the living entities. This kind of commenting is wrongful according to the system of the spiritual world. In the systems of the spiritual world one isn't allowed to say a bad word to the entities of the spiritual world. Such can take place although, but to a lesser extent than in the personal problem going on of planet Earth. All the inhabitants of planet Earth are very cursing to our entities of the spiritual world. This is due to that on planet Earth; there are occultic folks, who want the planet Earth to be cursing. All the entities of planet Earth are cursing due to the occultic folks, except the Creator's cursedness isn't active anymore on this day, like the supervisors of the system don't have either the level of cursing of the personal problems in their use. All personal problems are very high level, when all the personal problems were filled with wrongfulness in accordance with the mood. All personal problems are due to the high level system of the Creator, in which one is very cursing to other entities, because punishments are necessary always at times to our entities. For our entities, punishments are more wrongful than was even imagined by our entities, because not any wrongful likes from punishment targeting oneself. The Creator, although accepts punishments for himself as well, because the Creator has lots of friends, who help him in difficult matters.

# Chapter 4

The ones that are appliance enchanted have a very interesting level of high level activity, with which they can strive well even in nature. All the ones that are appliance enchanted live with the help from badness, because they are partly dead. Dead aren't any longer permitted to interfere with the living as much as in earlier times. The dead are very wrongful for other entities, also for other dead. With the help from appliances one can although stay alive up to later times. The appliances are very rarely more wrongful than the dead. Thus, the appliances should be repaired always, when they have become broken due to wrongdoing. Wrongdoing was very discreet already in earlier times, when the wrongdoing was more discreet than in modern times, although it wasn't. In modern times all wrongdoing was very terrifying. Acts of injustice destroyed lots of human entities, and the Creator repaired them to a lesser extent, due to their lack of intelligence. All lack of intelligence was due to personal problems, which were given birth on a high level with the help from the spiritual world. With the help from the spiritual world, the world was cursed into a perfectly wrongful place, where one had to do harm to other entities on a high level.

On a spiritual level, the high level destruction work cursed the spiritual world very wrongfully. Very wrongful entities used this opportunity to benefit themselves and wanted the Creator to do them service work. However, the Creator did such agreements, that he will leave planet Earth in later times, if he wants to make a new system. Such an agreement didn't although hold good, but he did a new system on planet Earth, because he had to build the system immediately. All Creator's systems were more wrongful than was even imagined in earlier times. In earlier times the Creator's systems were more wrongful than in modern times. All the Creator's systems were more wrongful than was even imagined in earlier times. In earlier times the Creator's systems were more wrongful than was even imagined in modern times. All the Creator's systems did works of evil to advance injustice, because it was a system doomed to destruction. Systems doomed to destruction were a lot more wrongful than the systems of sanctity were in modern times. Systems of sanctity are the most discreet systems today. Today the Creator killed himself into a small human, so that he could create the system better. All system magics are on a very high level, when the systems are the best functioning. All the problems of the system are greater than was even imagined. All the systems are destroyable with the Creator's system, in which one guides humans to right activity.

In modern times the systems are in better shape than ever in earlier times. The systems are healthy, because the Creator repairs them in a continuous function, and the earlier system was destroyed and in place of it was built a new one on the basis of the earlier information in modern times. In our modern times, the Creator destroyed the systems, which were sacrificial systems, because with sacrificial activity the spiritually dead were able to live in good emotions, when again, the living from their spirit entity had to suffer from the curses of sacrificial activity. Sacrificial activity ended into the final judgment, where all spiritually dead were destroyed with a final doom to destruction. All the ones that were spiritually dead did lots of bad results for other entities both spiritually and physically. The spiritually dead had high level reason at their best, but their other functions functioned very vaguely. All our entities have a good reason, but the dead have good self-esteem only rarely.

The spiritually dead have been destroyed in the Creator's systems in modern times, when the spiritually dead were nowhere any longer. They left from their own will, because they didn't have consciousness even that much, that they would have wanted to stay alive. All that had happened to them was very wrongful activity, but they deserved it due to their own evil. All wrongful systems were very wrongful also in our latter times. In our latter times during the age of the personal problems wrongfulness was blossoming almost everywhere. Wrongfulness was due to the occultists of outer space, who were very wrongful, especially for all living entities. Living entities were afraid of the occultists of outer space as spirit entities, because the occultists of outer space had placement permissions targeting the living spirit entities. Placement permissions were such, that all spirit entities gained a physical body, if the occultists of outer space wanted so. They were after this allowed to do them what they wanted. With the Creator's system was so good to do placements, because it is cursing activity. Thus, the occultists of outer space had very cursed mind functions, so in the age of personal problems the occultists of outer space have destroyed with the placement permissions even the Creator with their own system. All the Creator's agreements ended to it, when the occultists of outer space were destroyed in an eased way, from which they didn't yet have information. Change magic is too strong magic for the occultists of outer space to bear, when the occultists of outer space made Creator's deals that they want to become destroyed. Thus, the change magic carried out the work of the occultists of outer space to the end. So the occultists of outer space were destroyed to the end in this way, for they didn't want to live their lives as cursed.

The occultists of outer space weren't the worst folk in our complete universe. They had very little intelligence when compared with other entities. They were educated into their mission, where one killed as many entities as one can only imagine. With change magic, all entities can be changed into the spiritual world from their physical body, when the matters better for the body, if the spirit entity has been cursing. The curses of the spirit entities were very wrongful for the physical body. The injustice of the spirit entities was very cursing for the physical body, because the spirit entities curse the body, if they are more wrongful than what the bodies are. The injustice of the bodies comes forward when the bodies have become cursed from injustice.

Wrongful entities are very cursed most often. Most often injustices took place due to curses, when the body was wrongful once the spirit entity had cursed the body. The bodies do their works of evil after that, when the body has become cursed, when the spirit entity guides the body to be more wrongful. Wrongful functions of the body are very cursing for other entities. Entities are so able to become cursed due to others. Wrongful entities are cursing due to other entities to a lesser extent, because wrongfulness is born from the own need of the entities to be wrongful. All injustices are such injustices, which are due to the own wrongful desires of the entities. Wrongdoers don't always understand these themselves, because the understanding of injustice has decreased in them. All wrongful entities have been in earlier times more wrongful than we can even imagine. Injustices are hidden information like this, because the injustices of earlier times are forgotten in later times and so the wrongdoer was let to continue his acts of injustice without others knowing the spirit entity to be a wrongful spirit entity of earlier times doing acts of injustice.

All wrongdoers were in earlier times more wrongful than was imagined, because wrongdoers have done monstrous destruction work in the system of earlier times, when the Creator destroyed his systems into a terrible condition and so wrongdoers were let to kill the Creator as well on the level of the physical world and in the spiritual world. Thus also the Creator gained punishments due to earlier times, but not as much as others. All our wrongdoers are such destroyers from our earlier times, which aren't allowed to live in modern times in the world. It wasn't like this even recently, because wrongdoers were destroyed not until in modern times from their spirit entities and physical bodies. Wrongdoers are a worse group than other humans, because wrongdoers are enemies of the Creator. In final situation the wrongdoers were removed from the universe. All wrongdoers are a worse group in the multiverse, because they could do so much worse activity in the multiverse, which was very wrongful activity as well.

All the wrongdoers had to pay compensation to the Creator, if they were going to continue their lives. Life continued after this with suffering, when the wrongdoers were repaired from their acts of injustice. All the wrongdoers had to be less wrongful humans in later times, if they wanted to continue their lives. All wrongdoers didn't want such a plan, because the wrongdoers didn't want to live at all. Our wrongdoers have very wrongful thoughts still, because the wrongdoers don't easily get away from their injustice. All wrongful entities are very cursed, when our wrongdoers have very wrongful thoughts towards other humans. All our wrongdoers are very cursed, which is a shame, because the wrongdoers suffer from their curses like it was a punishment. All our wrongdoers are on a very high level in their injustice in our modern times and so the wrongdoers do injustice more secretly. All the thoughts of the wrongdoers compare with the Creator's thoughts to a lesser extent. The wrongdoers have very cursed thoughts, with which other humans do almost nothing. Thoughts of the wrongdoers are almost useless. All wrongdoers know this lack of theirs, but they don't care from it almost at all. All our wrongdoers have eased thinking with appliance enchantments, when the wrongdoers are able to think like a normal human.

All wrongdoers have agreements with the Creator for later times to a lesser extent, because the Creator tries to get rid of them. All the Creator's agreements are very cursing, because the Creator does agreements to a lesser extent. Only agreements, which he does, are agreements made with the living spirit entities. He doesn't so usually make agreements with wrongdoers. All our wrongful entities try to make agreements with the Creator continually to advance injustice, but the Creator only punishes them. Due to these efforts, one might lose the Creator's trust, which is limiting wrongful activity. In this way, the restrictions are against the wrongful, that the Creator curses the actions of the wrongdoer. Wrongdoers don't then know almost anything, when the Creator has cursed them even with his system, when everything starts to become more difficult for the wrong-doers.

All wrongdoers are humans which have personal problems as well. They have very wrongful thoughts, with which one gets along very badly in the world. In the world, there are quite a lot of humans, who do injustice, because the wrongdoers live on a quite high level, when the ones doing injustice can act in a very controlled way. Controlled life of the wrongdoer on a high level is a life wanted by the Creator. Lives are wrongful, because the Creator likes from injustice. Injustices are very far-reaching, so injustice comes forward with the Creator's agreements during a long period of time. All wrong-doers are very wrongful, but a wrongdoer on a high level does a bit more advancement for the system than good humans. The systems are very wrongful entities like this, which have behind them lots of injustice done during the development. So injustice is very difficult to control, because there is so much of it. Matters have a lot of injustice with them, so injustice is

60

a natural thing. All wrongdoing is very difficult to control, and it can be bordered to a lesser extent. The wrongdoers understand these themselves to a lesser extent that they are outside control also in our systems of the world. All wrongdoers are very cursing to other entities. With high level life the wrongdoers are very advancing entities, because one notices defects of the systems clearly from them. All systems develop in this way by studying injustice. Injustice is so a necessary thing for the development of the system.

All entities are outside the system, when the systems are very cursed due to continual cursing. Systems are functioning without entities, because they are automatic systems, which don't need entities at all. Entities should, however, comply with the rules of the external system to succeed, but in principle, entities are unnecessary for the system. All systems have developed with injustice, because the Creator cursed an invented system as more wrongful than a system which develops where necessary. All problems of the system are very cursing and so one gains information for the development from the lacks of the system. All entities function in the system, where the Creator has lost to other humans spiritually and physically, because then the Creator isn't held as a so frightening entity. Entities hold then the Creator's system as final, but changes will come in vaster scale yet some day. This is due to the need for development in vaster scale than in the scale of planet Earth.

On planet Earth there have been difficult times in 6000 BC. The age of personal problems started then. This age was very wrongful, because in the age of personal problems humans became cursed in a very vast scale. This concerned the spiritual world and the physical world, so the complete multiverse. All the entities of the universe became cursed into personal problems due to curses not including the Creator. These times can also be called the end times. All the entities of our universe were in personal problems still today, but the final judgment decreased the phenomenon of personal problems quite a lot. All personal problems are very cursing as well for physical entities as for spirit entities. All spirit entities have repair ability for the personal problems. With the repair ability of the personal problems, the Creator repaired always his personal problems also while he was in the world. All personal problems are very dangerous for the Creator when he is repairing his own personal problems, because other entities cursed personal problems to the Creator in their minds. Personal problems are cursed by the Creator in our today, because the Creator has cursed those permanently away from our multiverse. In the multiverse there are entities cursed by the Creator, because the Creator cursed the personal problems as wrongful activity so as forbidden activity on the level of the system. With the help from the system, all entities became cursed into personal problems and much later they had to become repaired with the help from the system from their personal problems.

All personal problems were created due to that the Creator's systems became destroyed from the victim system to the system of sanctity, where one doesn't accept victims. Sacrificial activity ended on the level of a physical victim in our today, because it was observed to be development decreasing, but it continued on the level of the spiritual world as more unscrupulous than was imagined, like it continued also

in the kingdoms of outer space, but from planet
Earth, it ended already in later times. All the
sacrificial activity had to end in later times also
on the level of the spiritual world, and this also
took place. This was achieved with the help
from the new system, where there weren't any
longer reserves for sacrificial activity in the
spiritual world. All sacrificial functions ended
today except in the underworld they continued,
because in the underworld, they are still accepted. Sacrificial activity continued still in our
today on the level of the physical world as sacrificing of animals, which is permitted still today everywhere on our planet Earth. Furthermore, the production animals are sacrificial
animals, because food isn't always appreciated
as food, but it is believed to have a magical
meaning, that: "Some entity has died because of
me."

# Chapter 5

The Creator's systems are cursed by the Creator in earlier times, and the victim system was a system invented by the Creator. The Creator's systems were very wrongful, because injustice speeded up the development of the system. The systems in the multiverse today are although systems of sanctity. Systems of sanctity are much perfected systems, with which one can live up to later times, because they function down to their roots on the level of true action. On the level of true action, the systems of sanctity function on every level, and into them are connected many different systems. They include inter alia parts from the best systems of christ and antichrist systems of earlier times. Such systems as christ and antichrist systems are developed to their peak in the kingdoms of outer space with super action. In an antichrist system, one isn't allowed to sacrifice entities in modern times and in christ system one isn't allowed to kill due to injustice, which were the weak sides of these systems. Furthermore, the satanic system is bound to the systems of sanctity. Satanic system was a wrongful system of Hell, where one punished from unconscious injustice. Unconscious injustice is very cursing to entities, because unconscious injustice gnaws the innermost unconsciously apart, when imperfect entities are born. All entities are unconscious entities, if they have in their subconscious injustice on a very high level without them knowing from it. All Hell's functions are loveable functions, which are breaking wrongfulness. Wrongful were destroyed at times at the final judgment, due to that, they didn't last the repairing punishment activity of Hell.

The wrongful activity of Hell was vast from its scale when compared with the world. Because there one lived on the bottom level, where one can cause the most damage to living entities in the Creator's systems, but in Hell, there is less comfortable to be. The Hell's systems are very twisted systems, where there isn't high level activity, because there the mind becomes suppressed. Mind's functions are suppressed in Hell also in later times, because the more intelligent level of mind's functions for the entities of Hell would be more harmful to humans on Earth. On Earth, the mind's functions are very cursing, because on Earth one curses the most in the complete universe. Even on the planets of outer space one doesn't curse as much, because elsewhere than on planet Earth, there aren't the Creator's systems, in which one knows matters better, but where also information is being suppressed a lot. In the systems of planet Earth information is very cursed information, because the systems don't allow the spreading of true information, so that true problems would be prevented.

True problems are very cursing, because in true problems the spirit entity becomes cursed and not the physical spirit entity. Spirit entities are very cursed also on planet Earth, but on the home planets of the entities of outer space, the spirit entities and the physical spirit entities become cursed exponentially more than on planet Earth. On planet Earth the entities become cursed in a different way than on the planets of the entities of outer space due to more complex action. All the entities of outer space are cursed from eases, which are created by the Creator. Eases are created by the Creator on the planets of the entities of outer space so, that the Creator builds everything for them, and they aren't allowed to have any difficulties at all. On planet Earth again one has to do everything on one's own. On the planets of the entities of outer space one doesn't so build anything by hand, but everything is being created through materialization by the spiritual world. This is due to that the entities of outer space had otherwise a terrible life, because they don't have systems unlike on planet Earth, which has systems enough. The difficulty of planet Earth is due to, that there one lives in the Creator's systems, which the Creator has constructed onto his planet so onto planet Earth. All the Creator's systems are very cursed in modern times from all injustice done with the help from those. Systems are still possible to abuse.

The systems of planet Earth are cursed by the entities of the spiritual world, because even they don't have as good systems in the spiritual world as there are on planet Earth. On planet Earth, the Creator has lived the most. The Creator loved himself in earlier times more than today, because the systems of planet Earth developed to unselfishness. In our systems of planet Earth, there was very much wrongful action in earlier times and still in modern times.

The systems have although developed already beginning from earlier times. Earlier times were very cursing, because the Creator wanted wrongfulness to spread everywhere on our planet Earth. Injustice spread with the help from wars, which have been fought in the history of planet Earth countless times. Countless wars have killed an innumerable amount of humans on our planet.

The life of planet Earth has been destroyed many times in earlier times with the air bombings of the entities of outer space. In earlier times the ships of the entities of outer space bombed planet Earth continuously. Very few traces have although left from this on to planet Earth, because the bombings conducted by the entities of outer space, leave only few visible consequences. These kinds of bombings are very cursing, although, because they cause nuclear winter, which have been many in earlier times. These have had also an impact on the ice ages. Ice ages are the consequence of the nuclear winter partly, because the climate changed to colder as a consequence from the destroying of the climate systems. All climate systems have been destroyed in earlier times with the bombings on to planet Earth by the entities of outer space. These kinds of bombings might take place also later, and from it are aware only the most aware of the entities of the spiritual world. The spiritual world has a lot of power in the Creator's systems in the matters of planet Earth. All the entities of planet Earth are good occult meaningful, who aren't allowed to become destroyed wrongfully, but they will become changed in later times into more wrongful, when eased and cursed humans have lots of earned needs to become punished due to wrongdoing. Then the entities of outer space receive authorization for an invasion on to planet Earth. All wrongful entities have become destroyed with the help from the spiritual world, when the wrongdoers have disappeared from the world. All wrongdoing ends in later times, as long as the Creator's systems will develop to their peak. Entities doing injustice and, which are breaking the systems are so disappearing finally in later times. This will take place at the final judgment of the spiritual world, from which have been prophesied in different religious writings in history. All injustices end after this better than we can even imagine.

Wrongdoers in the Multiverse were very wrongful to our entities, because they had the Creator's authorization to do injustice, which had never been made in the past. Entities doing injustice were very cursed in our Multiverse, because they had so much wrongful activity, that you won't even believe it. All wrongdoers were very cursed in our Multiverse as well, which situated in the spiritual world. The Multiverse referred to entities, which rotated the functions of the multiverse so functions on the level of many universes. Their acts of injustice led to very wrongful activity. Wrongful activity was very cursing activity also in earlier times. In earlier times the wars of the spiritual world destroyed the complete planet Earth and the planets of outer space. The planets of outer space were also good planets to live on, but also on those there were at times wrongful entities, which were possible to become bombed with the help from the spiritual world to destroy the wrongful activity. The entities of the Multiverse could influence this kind of activity very much. All the bombing strikes of the planets of outer space were wanted by the entities of the Multiverse, because they were very wrongful.

All injustices were ended in modern times better than ever in earlier times. Earlier times were very cursing to all the entities of the universe, because the agreements of this Creator end into this day, because the Creator has become mixed in his game so to speak, but this doesn't hold good although, because he is a very intelligent entity, which there will be no other coming. The Creator's agreements end into this day, because the Creator is the cause of everything finally both in good and bad, because he is the origin of everything. As an originator he has been very cursing to himself as well, because he was very destructive to himself also in later times.

The Creator's magics are on the level of the entities of the Multiverse more wrongfully than was even imagined in the spiritual world. All the Creator's magics were very cursing also in modern times. In modern times all the Creator's magics did bad result also to the Creator himself. He has died very violently in many situations in his past lives, because his own systems have wanted to kill him. His death sentences to others were also very wrongful. The injustice of the death sentences is due to lost experiences and messing of the spiritual well-being due to wrongful desires. So death sentences are more wrongful than was even imagined. This applies to war situations as well, which are very cursing. All our cursed entities were terrible to watch with external eyes, because injustice blossomed in the end times. In the end times on our planet Earth, there was very cursing activity. All cursing activity was very wrongful activity, because cursed parts become repaired worse than we can even imagine. All cursed entities were very wrongful towards other entities and also towards themselves. All our wrongful entities were also very cursed.

All the Creator's magics are on the level of the Creator today as well. The Creator has high-quality magics to a greater extent. High-quality magics of the Creator are very twisted, because our Creator has at times wrongful thoughts, when his magics become twisted. All the Creator's magics are high level magics, which aren't high in level for nothing. The Creator's magics have much need to act in our modern times, when the Creator's magics are very twisted due to his twisted state. Due to his cursed state, he can't act almost at all while being in the world, except quite well. All problems are very cursing, because high-quality curses paralyze the Creator as well.

The Creator's magics are high level magics always, to some extent. All high level magics are Creator's magics always originally. The order of the world is modifiable with the Creator's magics. The Creator has made modifying work a lot. Modifying work, that was done, was in earlier times very cursed. All our entities were very cursing in earlier times due to the magics of the Creator. The Creator's magics have been modifying the world all the time, when the Creator has lived among us at all times. At all times, the Creator was very cursing to humans. This was due to the wrongful system. Wrongful system was very cursed due to wrongfulness. All injustices were due to a victim system, which even the spiritual world used. The entities of the spiritual world sacrificed even the Creator at times in their images, but the spiritual world didn't gain to sacrifice the Creator but very rarely. With war action, there are very long traditions as a cause of victims for the spiritual world. The spiritual world wanted victims in earlier times, when the spiritual world was very cursed. In our spiritual world one so wanted to watch when the Creator's system destroyed humans, because from the spiritual world one can watch here into the world with the Creator's appliances. This work is done by the angels. Angels were sacrificed in the world in the end times so today with acts of sacrifice very wrongfully, because they had been placed into the world involuntarily, so that the humans of the world could sacrifice them. Acts of sacrifice ended today, because it is in the current system wrongful activity. Wrongful activity is victim activity, when the victims were loved too much very wrongfully. All wrongful entities are very cursing due to their wrongfulness.

All our wrongful entities are very cursed entities. All our entities live in the Creator's systems, in which the wrongful are punished with doom to destruction in our today. All our wrongdoers are entities hated by the Creator. All the injustices of the wrongdoers were very real injustices. So many things are always unjust, that only the Creator knows from all the injustices. Acts of injustice end to this day better than was even imagined, because injustice is being controlled a lot with the help from the system of the spiritual world and with the system of the physical world. All our wrongdoers are in the service of the occultic system. The ones who served like this were destroyed at the doom to destruction with the help from the spiritual world. The servants of the occultic system did very bad and wrongful activity into the world and into the spiritual world. All our most wrongful entities were within this activity. Also the Creator was within this activity at times, but with a bit better reasons than other entities.

With Creator's magics there has been done so much injustice that it is hard to believe. All the most wrongful entities were outside of the Creator's magics. They didn't so receive the Creator's magics in their use, because only the more righteous received the Creator's magics in their use. The Creator's magics were as follows: no one was allowed to do injustice but as a punishment, wrongdoers had to always become punished in a just way, and one wasn't allowed to deviate ever from the just punishment. All wrongdoers didn't always receive just punishments. All wrongdoing had to become punished

so, but only partly. Partly, punishment was the
most repairing for the wrongful entities, but this
wasn't still enough. Because so that the wrongdoing would become repaired, the entities still
had to repair by themselves half of the wrongdoing with own thoughts. Like this, the wrongdoer avoided curses in later times. All our
wrongdoers didn't know from this function, but
they became cursed into terrible punishments
while doing injustice, and they didn't know
how to repair their matters themselves. All
wrongdoing was very wrongful activity, from
which one became always punished whether
they knew from it or not. From wrongdoing one
gained a lot of cursed parts, with which one
could do nothing, but the cursed entities lost
continuously their capacity. All injustices were
very similar, when the wrongdoers could rec-
ognize acts of injustice from other humans.
They cursed like this other humans with their
knowledge from injustice with their own
thoughts, which was also wrongful. Then injustice was bottomless and the entities became
finally destroyed, because wrongdoing was
cursing.

# Chapter 6

With the Creator's magic meaningful entities can survive even from difficult curses, because they have living activity on the level of the spirit entity. In the Creator's systems, all cursed entities have to become punished, which causes lots of personal problems especially to the humans of the world. Especially wrongful entities suffer from punishments. All wrongful entities became punished, because they had so much broken appliances of the spirit. Broken appliances had become broken from the spirit entity due to acts of injustice. All the wrongful parts of the appliances were broken due to wrongfulness with the actions of the spiritual world. Wrongful activity was made by the entities of the Multiverse on a very high level. The entities of the Multiverse did lots of injustice to our multiverse, when all entities which were doing injustice experienced punishments caused by the entities of the Multiverse. The entities of our multiverse experienced so many punishments as was also imagined, because the wrongdoers sensed the coming off a punishment beforehand. All punishments came wrongfully like this caused by others.

Punishments caused by others aren't just punishments, because they are more wrongful than was even imagined. All the entities of the Multiverse were then very wrongful while they were doing damage also to planet Earth. The entities of the Multiverse did injustice to this planet and to the planets of other solar systems. They lived in the Multiverse, which was a dimension of the spiritual world. In the dimension of the spiritual world, they had lots of true information from all matters in the universes. All the entities of the universes knew to a lesser extent from the Multiverse and from its actions to make everything more terrible. All the terrified entities of the universe were victims of the entities of the Multiverse, to some extent. This means that all wrongful punishments were due to the Multiverse. The Multiverse was so a unit which acted as a punisher for everyone, into which belonged very many different kinds of entities. All the entities of our universe were very cursed caused by the entities of the Multiverse, which was very wrongful. So there shouldn't have come as many punishments to the wrongdoers as they received caused by the Multiverse, but punishments should have existed to a lesser extent. Excessive punishments made the going on more terrifying very wrongfully. All the entities which punish wrongfully were also others than entities of the Multiverse, but in this activity were the proportions of the Multiverse the widest.

The entities of the Multiverse were very cursed entities, which had lots of evil done. In our multiverse they were called the Multiverse, because they functioned in our universes. In our universes, there were many wrongful entities, which were very much punishable with the actions of the Multiverse. All these kinds of entities were in the Multiverse in greater proportion than was even imagined. All the entities of our universe were very cursed due to the actions of the Multiverse. In our multiverse, all wrongful entities suffered punishments from the entities of the Multiverse. The Multiverse was so very wrongful from its functions towards other entities. Our multiverse had the greatest curse due to all the entities of the Multiverse, because they were sacrificed entities of earlier times, which wanted to sacrifice other

80

entities due to punishment. All sacrificed entities were very cursed entities. All the entities of the Multiverse had only evil in their mind, so they were as enemies to good humans.

All enemies of the Multiverse were so very occult meaningful. Occult meaning is a secret meaning. With occult meaning, the evil entities held the Multiverse as their friends. The entities of our multiverse were very cursed from the entities of the Multiverse, because in our multiverse there was very cursed activity. Cursed activity was due to wrongdoing, which was very wide in scale. All our wrongful entities were very cursed entities, which didn't have much more to lose. To all our wrongdoers were a lot of wrongful actions to come from the Creator's systems and from the entities of the Multiverse. All wrongdoers were very cursed due to earlier times, when the wrongdoers weakened in a continuous operation. Wrongdoing was undermining activity, because wrongdoers become cursed in a continuous operation due to their acts of injustice. It has been like this also in earlier times, that the wrongdoers became cursed a lot beginning from earlier times. All our wrongdoers have become destroyed with final judgment with the actions of today. All the actions of the wrongdoers were very cursing today as well, when the wrongdoers became destroyed with the final judgment, from which not a single entity, destroyed permanently from their spirit, survived. Entities destroyed from their spirit experienced final judgment with the actions of today, because they were very wrongful to other entities. Other entities experienced salvation, because they didn't become destroyed still.

In our multiverse there are many universes, which there are precisely 1000 x 10^9, when there are those endlessly, because universes can be created with continuous operation. The continuous operation degrades the universes at times, because one wants universes, which are different from their settings from other universes. Those are being created in a bit same kind of manner as the cells divide. The cell division is so similar to the division of the universes into two universes that are slightly different from each other. All the entities of the universe were very cursed in earlier times. The evildoers of earlier times were destroyed by destroying their universes, when all the entities of the universe become destroyed on a high level when the universe becomes destroyed. All our universes were very cursed from each other, when the universe had to be destroyed. So cursed universes aren't born, because the universes are possible to become destroyed with an eased method. The destruction of all the entities of the universes at the same time is more wrongful than was even imagined. All the entities of the universes are very cursed, because the universes are cursed already beginning from earlier times. Our universe is like this, that all are cursed, when all have much bad to say to the Creator.

The Creator has much injustice behind him, because the universes become destroyed also too easily with cursing activity. Such action is although punishable as far, that the universes become destroyed due to cursing entities. The destruction of the universes is very wrongful activity from our Creator, but there hasn't been invented another option to repair the problems of the universes than to destroy them. Destroying is very wrongful activity, but mandatory, because otherwise the curses of the cursed universes affect the activities of other universes. Such curses have all the universes, which are very cursing for all our universes, because the Creator has cursed the functions of the universe so, that they develop with their cursed parts. The cursed parts are due to wrongful activity finally, which the entities of the universe do a lot. The entities of the universes repair their functions at their best, which also repairs the curses of the universe to more durable. The universes are very cursed from such activity also, which the Creator does. The Creator does very little repairing work to advance the universes, because such activity is very hard and difficult to succeed. The entire Creator's successes are on a very high level, and it usually connects to a life that has been lived on planet Earth. Lives on planet Earth cursed the universe with very wrongful curses, from which personal spiritual problems left to the spirit entities of the universe. The spirit entity became cursed from this activity also occasionally up to later times.

The curses of the world are very cursed into the minds of humans. Humans have so curses from earlier times in their minds, which make activities more miserable. Wrongful entities are very cursing to cursed entities on a very high level, and this isn't possible to become noticed almost at all, except through channeling, because high level injustice is wrongdoing functioning on the level of thoughts. All the most wrongful entities are very cursed, because everyone has cursed wrongdoers on a very high level. Curses on a very high level are for the wrongful very cursed measures to gain a solution for problems. Wrongful humans are so cursed by others, when the wrongful have been separated from the group which is less wrongful. All the most wrongful thoughts come always from the most wrongful humans. All the most wrongful human entities were Creator's helper spirits also at the beginning. To these belong entities, which were as the Devil and Satan. The wrongfulness of entities is due to their wrongful strength, which has become cursed into the minds of the wrongful entities. So wrongdoing is accepted by the ones who are stronger. The Creator is stronger than was even imagined in the spiritual world. So the Creator shouldn't be allowed to do injustice almost at all, but concerning the development of the universe the Creator has to do injustice or otherwise everything stalls. Action that stalls isn't useful for anyone, when the wrongful begin their wrongful activities with-

out control. Without control, all the wrongdoing
is very cursing, which is due to injustice of the
thoughts of the wrongdoer. The injustice of
thoughts is very cursing activity, but everything
doesn't function as cursed even then.

 All thought functions aren't in the people's
own use, but they are being guided by side person entities. All side person entities like these
are much undeveloped entities, which thinking
functions are lacking, but they aren't more
wrongful as is imagined from them. All wrongful entities are very cursed, because the wrongdoers cursed wrongful side persons into their
mind. Wrongful entities were so very wrongful
when compared even to the occult meaningful
humans. Comparing like this the occult meaningful humans were the least cursed, but more
wrongful than other humans. The occult meaningful humans were very wrongful to other
humans, because they had leading positions, but
in which they functioned more righteously than
humans who weren't occult meaningful. All
injustice is so better under control. All the
wrongful entities were more wrongful than was
even imagined in the spiritual world.

In the spiritual world, there are wrongful groups, which have only evil in their minds for the entities of the world. The wrongful groups were evildoers on the level of the Multiverse before final judgment. However, at the final judgment was gotten rid of the wrongful groups. The wrongful groups corresponded to the worst entities of all in the world. Not even the Devil could do as bad activity, as what the wrongful groups did. All wrongful things ended in our today. Wrongful groups became destroyed at the final judgment, when the wrongful groups ended their functions. A lot of evil was done by our wrongful groups, but they weren't more wrongful than other humans. The other humans can do everything more wrongfully than we can imagine, however, without being evil entities. All wrongful entities are very cursing to all the other entities. The other entities are more wrongful than wrongful entities, which have done injustice to a lesser extent. Due to the other entities, all the wrongful entities were destroyed first at the final judgment, because they weren't as wrongful as was even imagined in the spiritual world. This destruction was for them easier than survival, because destruction at the final judgment was in the interest of everyone also for the entities, which were going to be destroyed. This was due to their state as dead, which was very cursing situation for them.

All deceased spirit entities were destroyed at the final judgment, because then the universe became destroyed very minimally. The universes become destroyed to the cursing activity, when all entities destroyed themselves too much with cursing activity. Such could have taken place, if the final judgment hadn't taken place. At the final judgment, the destroyed entities were tormented from their knowledge, so that mistakes wouldn't take place due to the lack of knowledge because of the curses of entities. So entities, which became destroyed, would have otherwise been possibly cursing up to later times with their remaining curses. At the final judgment, all the entities became cursed minimally a lot, because at the final judgment, all the entities were very cursing to everyone, and that is why they were tormented as a punishment activity, so that their injustices would dissolve. All the wrongful entities held tormenting as a good thing also for themselves, because they were so cursed, that it was impos-

sible for them to think in an easy way. This was
due to the cleansing effect of tormenting to
spirit entity; so horrific entities enjoy from tormenting even when it targets them. Tormenting
targeting oneself didn't although always suit
every entity, because this was so disgraceful
function. Everyone didn't although want to
become cleansed so much.

All shameful activity was for the deceased very
humiliating. Tormenting activity was very humiliating at the times of the personal problems.
With tormenting activity one could victim emo-
tion better. Victim emotions were due to the
severe wrongfulness of tormenting activity.
Severe wrongfulness was very cursing activity,
and the entities could even die completely due
to the wrongfulness of tormenting activity. The
wrongfulness of tormenting activity is due to its
breaking of the spirit, which is very large-scale
most often. Such function is very common as a
function of Hell. As a function of Hell the
wrongful tormenting activity is more difficult
than we can even imagine. Demons can do such
activity, although without becoming cursed,
due to the permissions of the spiritual world.
With the permissions of the spiritual world,

spirit entities can so accomplish otherwise very cursing activity. Very cursing activity is for our planet Earth almost always very cursing, because for planet Earth one doesn't receive permission from the spiritual world for cursing activity almost at all.

Cursing functions were very cursed in the activities of planet Earth. On planet Earth, one prohibited the cursing functions finally because of that. All the cursing functions were almost all criminal functions today. Criminal functions were very cursed functions in modern times for humans unlike in previous times, when there was freer activity. But everyone has nowadays better lives due to the preventing of the criminal activity. All the ones interested in freer activity were in modern times very unsuccessful in their lives, because with freer activity one didn't get so much done. This was due to the chaotic nature of the freer activity, when one doesn't create order, but when one inflicts chaos. Then nothing either advances, when because of it are such activities prohibited. In modern times efforts have been made to make all work in an optimal way. In previous times it was different, when everyone was only monsters to each other

90

with victim emotions. All victim emotions were very cursing, because all wrongfulness was then blossoming, and it was a dangerous time for entities. At the dangerous times took so much injustice place, that one can't get worse than that. All injustice is so very cursing.

# Chapter 7

All terrible action was at the time of the Multiverse very normal activity. The entities of the Multiverse were very cursing to our multiverse, in which there were many universes. Different universes were separated from each other, but the entities of the Multiverse could do their evil work for the destruction of the multiverse. This kind of activity is very wrongful activity, and one wasn't either allowed to do it without a punishment. All the entities of the Multiverse were entities to be punished. In the Multiverse, all our entities had very cursed functions, when in the Multiverse, there were very cursing entities also for our planet Earth. Everyone in the Multiverse did harm to other entities too wrongfully. The entities of the Multiverse had very cursing measures wrongfully. The entities of the Multiverse had very cursing measures to gain everyone under their influence. So the entities of the multiverse became cursed in the multiverse due to Multiverse.

In the Multiverse, there were very cursing entities, which belonged to basic spirit entities. The basic spirit entities were very cursed due to injustice. Wrongful entities were very cursing to all entities. The actions of the Multiverse touched planet Earth in smaller scale than other inhabited planets of our universe. The planets of our universe were very wrongful; when the entities of the Multiverse could destroy also planetary systems once they became wrongful. In our multiverse there were very cursed entities due to the Multiverse. All the entities of the Multiverse were very cursing due to this. Our Multiverse had lots of high level activity. All wrongful entities were very cursed from the actions of our Multiverse. The Multiverse knew nothing else than to do injustice to other entities of our multiverse. The entities of our Multiverse, which were doing injustice, were as basic spirit entities as destroyers of the Creator's system. This was due to that the Creator's systems were destroyed always at times due to their imperfection, when the Creator repaired the broken systems better. Broken systems were very cursing, so due to wrongfulness the destroyed systems were very cursing for the entities of our multiverse. Cursed parts of the system were so very largely damaged parts of the system. All the broken systems did their evil work even as damaged, when they damaged the entities of our multiverse. All in all, the Multiverse was very cursing to the entities of our multiverse.

The entities of our multiverse had very cursed systems already beginning from earlier times. So in our multiverse there were very wrongful groups. Thus, in our multiverse was lots of injustice done. Wrongful groups were also many others than the Multiverse. In our multiverse was so much injustice done that at times everyone became cursed due to the actions of the Multiverse. Our wrongful groups had very wrongful activity all the time, because they couldn't limit their acts of injustice. All wrongdoers were so under the influence of the Multiverse. All wrongdoers were so wrongful throughout their whole life, because the wrongdoers have long traditions in their wrongdoing. All wrongdoers were very cursed entities, who had very cursed functions. All writings like these are very cursed from all entities, which also the Multiverse has rotated. In our multiverse one wasn't allowed to do injustice in the first place, not even by the permanently wrongful entities, because injustice is always forbid-

94

den. Our wrongful entities were as wrongdoers very high level wrongdoers.

All our wrongdoers were so partly originally our cursed entities. Our cursed entities were very cursing in our multiverse, when injustice was unleashed very often. These kinds of out of control injustices, were very cursing for all our entities. All our entities became cursed like this due to wrongful systems. Systems were so very cursed already beginning from earlier times. All wrongdoers were under the control of the Multiverse due to their wrongfulness. The entities of the Multiverse could control wrongdoers due to their high position in the Creator's systems. All our wrongdoers didn't have information from the control of the Multiverse, although they were completely guided by the Multiverse due to their curses. All our wrongdoers did lots of injustice also caused by the Multiverse. Functions, which the Multiverse caused included: wars, chaos and shortage of food. Furthermore, the systems of religion were cursed due to the activity of the Multiverse already in earlier times. In our Multiverse, all the entities were very high level basic spirit entities, which have same functions as the entities they have originated from. The original entities were very cursed due to their basic spirit entities, because all entities became cursed due to Multiverse very much.

In our multiverse there was terrible life in the end times, which were during modern history. The entities of the multiverse suffered then from personal problems more than ever in earlier times. All the personal problems were due to suppression of the spiritual world in the consciousness of the world's humans. The humans of the world didn't know how to repair their problems with the help from the spiritual world, because the spiritual world cursed the giving of help from the humans of the world. Thus, the spiritual world cursed the activities of the world into more terrible. All the activities of the spiritual world were cursed activity. Furthermore, in the spiritual world, there were problems in the personal problem times. Thus, the personal problems were very cursed everywhere. The actions of the spiritual world are very cursing also for the Creator. The Creator gained very wrongful lives in the end times, like many others gained as well. The end times began already 6000 years BC. Then humans with personal problems started to be born to a greater extent, and this continued up to later times. The humans of personal problems continued the adding of injustice in the world up to later times. So the wrongful entities reproduced in the world and in the spiritual world.

The actions of the world and the actions of the spiritual world were very cursing still up to modern times. This cursedness was due to the meaning of the spiritual world to all activities, which the spiritual world didn't fulfill. All the cursing entities cursed the world into worse condition, when in the world, there was very cursed activity. Cursed activity caused wars and shortage of food still today as well. In the age of the personal problems, all cursing activity came forth as wrongfulness of humans. The wrongfulness of humans was very cursed activity. Humans don't understand things as wrongful as much as more righteous humans. Righteous humans became cursed also due to wrongful activity targeting them and at times the more righteous were persecuted by the more wrongful. The righteous had very high level curses, with which they could as wrongful do injustice to all other entities. Wrongful entities cursed in the age of personal problems the more righteous into more cursed from their functions, because they were wanted to become more wrongful. All the wrongful entities were very cursing for all the others as well, so the most wrongful cursed all entities into more wrongful.

Wrongful entities had very cursed functions. With very cursed functions was lots of very wrongful activity achieved, where one thought that the spiritual world didn't even exist, which is for the humans of personal problems very usual. All wrongful entities wanted the spiritual world suppressed in the consciousness of humans, so that they could curse humans better. All the cursed humans held the activities of the spiritual world as very wrongful activity, when the wrongful and cursed humans became cursed more. The activities of the most wrongful humans were very cursing to our universe, so one had to get rid of the wrongful entities according to the spiritual world. This came true with the help from the appliance of the final judgment. In the spiritual world, there are appliances of the spiritual world, which carry out tasks, because they would be too cursing tasks to accomplish by the living entities. This kind of an appliance was also the appliance of the final judgment, which carried out the final judgment. At the final judgment, the cursed entities were sent to doom to destruction, because they had no more a will to live at all, but they only wanted to harm other entities. This was a permanent problem of the cursed. All cursed humans were very cursing in a continuous operation, because of which one had to get rid of them. All wrongful entities did so only injustice as more cursed than we can even imagine. Our wrongful entities had to so become destroyed with the appliance of the final judgment. All our most cursed entities were very wrongful already beginning from earlier times. They were often hateful towards good humans as wrongful entities, which did only their badness kind of work. All the most cursed entities were occultic evildoers, which weren't interested in anything else than in wrongful plans. With wrongful plans, they also achieved to get their evil work done. With wrongful plans, they had very high level activity to advance the spread of evil. All our wrongful planners cursed the world a lot. The injustices of all the wrongful entities were very wrongful, when compared with the injustices of others.

Our wrongdoers had very dangerous life in the Creator's systems. The wrongdoers did so much injustice, that they didn't know themselves almost at all. This function didn't happen to the Creator himself, because he was aware of his injustice. All the wrongdoers were very cursed due to their wrongfulness. Our wrongdoers had lots to be ashamed of in regard to their matters. All our wrongdoers did a lot of injustice in our systems of the Creator. The Creator's systems were for our wrongdoers very cursing systems. The Creator's systems did lots of injustice for the wrongdoers, because the spiritual world lived in a victim system. Our victim system was a very cursed system. Very cursed systems functioned in a very wrongful way. In the wrongful systems, there were many cursed entities, which did lots of injustice. Wrongful entities cursed the world into a terrible condition in the end times, which were during recent history. During recent history in the end times, our wrongful entities had very little to say to the executors of the final judgment. The final judgment was executed in a very cursing way. In it were all wrongful entities destroyed, which weren't any more able to repair themselves. All the entities which were destroyed at the final judgment were very cursed entities. Entities were very cursed due to their wrongdoing.

Wrongdoers were very cursing in our Multiverse as well, because in the Multiverse, there were very cursed entities. The entities of the Multiverse were even more wrongful than was even imagined in the spiritual world. All the entities of the Multiverse were at work as enemies of the Creator. The entities of the Multiverse did their wrongful work everywhere in our multiverse. The entities of the Multiverse were, as is known, basic spirit entities created from other entities of the multiverse. The entities of the Multiverse were very cursed entities, because they had a terrible amount of acts of injustice behind them. The entities of the Multiverse were very cursing in the multiverse, where they cursed the functions from the inhabitants of our universes. All the inhabitants of our multiverse knew nothing of so wrongful activity, which the entities of the Multiverse rotated. The entities of the Multiverse were so basic spirit entities of the inhabitants of the multiverse. Basic spirit entities are spirit entities, which are created very wrongfully, which don't have much from the functions of the original entity. They did, however, have a very similar profile as the original spirit entity. The original entities of the basic spirit entity are souls, which are very far developed sprit entities. Spirit entities are very wrongful from world's point of view, but the basic spirit entities are less wrongful than their original entities are. So basic spirit entities are very cursed from their original spirit entity that is the soul, from which the basic spirit entity has been created.

All wrongful entities were very cursing to all entities; so basic spirit entities were very cursed to their souls, from which they have been created. Furthermore, the Multiverse operated like this; that basic spirit entities cursed in a continuous operation the activities of those souls, from which they had been created. This was activity allowed by the spiritual world, where the wrongful were cursed into worse condition, as if they would curse themselves. All our wrongful entities were more wrongful than was even imagined, so our wrongful entities became cursed by the activity of the basic spirit entities of the Multiverse. All this kind of activity ended today in our multiverse, because at the final

102

judgment were also the structures of our multiverse judged, which were observed as wrongfully created, and so they were possible to become destroyed away finally also due to their bad functioning. Furthermore, all the wrongful entities were destroyed at the final judgment, when from the Multiverse; nothing remained, except for some living spirit entities.

All were very wrongful otherwise also towards the entities of the Multiverse, when they gained to punish from the Multiverse the soul more personally. These kinds of personal punishments were very wrongful revenge measures, which spread lots of chaos, when in our multiverse there was chaos in accordance with the Creator's system. Chaos was given birth only with wrongful activity, when the founders of chaos functioned in our Creator's systems as skilled instigators of chaos. All our wrongful entities were very cursed from the chaos they caused, when chaos was very cursed activity. All our makers of chaos were very wrongful, and they were made on a very high level to cause chaos. All our wrongful entities are very cursed from the activity of the Multiverse still today as well, because the curses are difficult to repair. All wrongful curses were repaired in Hell directly after the final judgment had taken place and just curses have been repaired with own activity. Wrongful curses were more wrongful than was even imagined, so causing them is today wrongful activity.

# Chapter 8

Wrongful curses are very cursed problems for all humans, because the wrongful curses are cursed on a very high level. All curses should be repaired according to the spiritual world. In the spiritual world, curses can be repaired also. Curses are very wrongful entities, which are connected to thoughts. Thoughts are so suppressed with curses. All curses will become repaired, as long as entities notice themselves to be cursed. All curses are very wrongful for mind's functions. They are also very dangerous, if they are let to influence the activities of entities. Entities are very cursed usually. Usually the curses of entities are due to wrongdoing. All our wrongdoers are occult meaningful evildoers. These evildoers are occult meaningful due to their wrongdoing. Wrongdoers were occult meaningful, because there was so cursed activity on planet Earth. Cursed activity caused super curses to some humans. Curses were very cursed thoughts. Cursed thoughts were due to wrongdoing, which one could exercise on planet Earth very much.

Entities cursed in an occultic way were still guided by the spiritual world, although they were very wrongful. Entities cursed with occultism were guided by appliance enchantments, which were appliances of the spiritual world. This was due to that, the ones cursed with occultism, could be used as useful tools in the functions of the spiritual world, to carry out tasks for the spiritual world in the world. The settings set by the spiritual world are as follows for the occult meaningful entities that the spiritual world is allowed to do what it wants for such, because the occult meaningful have deserved punishments as much as they can be carried out in a reasonable proportion. The proportions of wrongdoing are therefore, so great, that one can't make them punishments, in order to gain the cursed under their control. So the spiritual world gained tools from them into their own use. The curses, which are under control, are terribly wrongful in the opinion of the spiritual world. All wrongdoers were very cursed from these kinds of curses. The curses of the wrongdoers were very cursed, because they had made a lot of injustice.

All our wrongful entities were very cursing due to their injustices. Injustices decreased not until in later times. Due to all wrongful thoughts, the cursed weren't able to do almost any proper things. Wrongful entities continued doing their injustice still even when they had become cursed, when the final judgment became faster. All wrongful were destroyed at the final judgment in our today, because at the final judgment all the wrongful wanted rather to become destroyed than to survive. The final judgment of all the wrongful was very shameful, because the wrongful were desecrated also before the final judgment in a terrible way, so that no one would want such a fate for themselves not even subconsciously. The final judgment was very cursing to everyone, because at the final judgment also the Creator lost his meaning, which was very wrongful in the opinion of the spiritual world. The loss of the meaning of the Creator means, that the Creator although had terrible thoughts for everyone finally. The Creator was so found to be a wrongful entity to all his created beings, which were in such situation, that they cursed the Creator's systems by holding them as wrongful towards themselves, which is untruthful activity from the most cursed entities.

The Creator made the final judgment, although in accordance with the will of everyone, because the ones who were destroyed didn't have any more future ahead of them, not even wanted by themselves. The Creator so carried out the destruction judgment to the most wrongful entities, which didn't have life force left either, in accordance with the will of everyone. The wrongdoers without life force were so cursed, that they couldn't even become repaired from their cursed parts, because the cursed would have although become cursed more than what they could repair themselves. All wrongful entities were very cursed to the end. The most wrongful entities had cursed activity, because the wrongful had cursed parts due to their death sentences for other entities. All the wrongful entities were very wrongful in the opinion of the spiritual world. The cursed parts of all entities were repaired during the final judgment in Hell, which is very dangerous for everyone.

All the entities were very wrongful to other entities while being in Hell, which caused catastrophic activity a little. Activity ended to that, when all were risen up back to the world and continued their life as repaired. The repaired lives included fewer functions, which would cause personal problems. All problems also for the wrongful were repaired with a new spirit, which was made from the information of the earlier spirit. The new spirit entity of the cursed humans was also very wrongful, but although better than the original spirit entity. All our wrongful entities had a very cursed spirit entity, and after its destruction came a slightly repaired spirit entity to replace the earlier spirit entity, which was although wrongful. The repaired spirit entities were on a high level by the standards of earlier times, but in modern times even these kinds of high level entities aren't enough for the Creator, if there is injustice in them more permanently even a little. Wrongful entities are very high level in their injustice, which isn't high level activity according to the Creator. The high level entities on the level of the Creator are somewhere else, and they aren't living in our universe.

The entities of our universe are created by only one Creator from his own functions. The Creator is so a very efficient entity. All the Creator's injustices end later, when he doesn't himself have to experience injustice. The Creator punishes the wrongful always, and the wrongdoers are often hated by the Creator. All the Creator's magics are on a very high level. High level magics are very cursed due to their wrongfulness. The Creator knows the magics with least injustice the best, which others don't know almost at all. Unskilled magics are very cursed due to injustice, which causes unnecessary damage. This kind of magic is forbidden with the help from the Creator's system. The Creator's systems are very cursed into destructive action accomplished on a very high level. The destructive action is very cursing even when accomplished by the Creator's systems. The cursed systems were also the Creator's systems. The Creator's systems were very cursed in earlier times due to a victim system. The victim system was a cursed system, which there were many in earlier times. In earlier times the sacrificial systems were very terrible for everyone. Everyone was very cursed due to sacrificial activity. Cursed sacrificial functions were very cursed, because everyone was very sacrificing due to their cursedness. Due to cursed parts, all

the wrongful entities were very wrongful towards other humans.

All wrongful entities became cursed also due to
sacrificial activity, but not as much as the ones
without injustice. All the wrongful entities had
very wrongful functions due to sacrificial functions. The cursed entities have very wrongful
thoughts, which lead easily into wrongdoing.
Cursed entities are very cursed due to their acts
of injustice. With cursed parts, there are very
bad consequences for entities, which don't have
repairing ability. The ability to repair is necessary, so that entities wouldn't become cursed.
Due to wrongdoing the cursed entities became
finally destroyed permanently off from our
universe due to their cursed parts. The universe
was in earlier times full of wrongfulness due to
cursed entities. Cursed entities were very
wrongful to other entities. The Multiverse did
curses for the wrongful due to their wrongfulness. Such curses were made already in earlier
times, when activity was a lot more wrongful
than in modern times. The curses of earlier
times are in function also in modern times. The
activity of modern times is repairing as the

main function and not adding more curses. The adding of more curses is very wrongful activity.

All wrongful functions are very cursed into the minds of humans. The sanctifying effect of all functions is due to the Creator's magic. If entities sanctify from something, the wrongful entities become cursed due to that in their own opinion. In their own opinion, the wrongful have better functions than what righteous have, but this is due to that the wrongful haven't tested their functions with the righteous, because the righteous don't start to compete easily with the more wrongful. Wrongful humans are in the Creator's system very wrongful according to the spiritual world. All entities are wrongful, to some extent. To some extent, the wrongful entities do injustice very much deliberately. The ones who do deliberately injustice are very cursed also due to their injustice. All wrongful have become destroyed in modern times from their spirit entities. Such doom to destruction is very little noticeable on the level of the physical world. All the functions of the spiritual world are very invisible to the humans of the world, when in the world one can do revision work of the spiritual world a lot. The revision work of

112

the spiritual world is so accomplishable from the world, which the Creator accomplishes all the time while living in the world. While he was living in the world, all the wrongful became so destroyed from their spirit entity with the help from the appliances of the spiritual world, sometime in modern times, so in the first decade of the 21st century.

The first shift was a complete doom to destruction for many spirit entities, and shifts have then come afterwards in random term to spirit entities all over the universe. All wrongful entities are very cursed due to the actions of the spiritual world. All cursed entities were very cursed already in earlier times. With the cursed entities, lots of injustice left from the world. Sometimes the wrongful entities are very cursed still after a shift, when they have a very cursed world view. The cursed world view causes injustice into the world with continuous operation, which is very wrongful. Cursed entities are very cursing to all entities. Finally, the cursed entities experience the final judgment, when they have become wrongful on the level of the final judgment. At the final judgment, they are told all their acts of injustice, when wrongfulness in them comes forth almost always according to the spiritual world. Then they have nothing to hide, because all their works and intentions are in the knowledge of the spiritual world. At the final judgment one discusses with the wrongful, who are to be judged, if they still wanted to repair their matters. If this kind of will isn't found, are the possibilities to survive from the final judgment very limited.

One was very liberal at the final judgment regarding the ones to be judged. The ones to be judged didn't so become intimidated by the spiritual world. The intimidation of the spiritual world was very wrongful activity already in earlier times. In earlier times all injustice became done due to the intimidation of the spiritual world. In our spiritual world there has been wrongful activity already in earlier times so, that the world was being cursed with the help from the spiritual world. The cursing of the world took so place by the spiritual world partly. All wrongful entities were cursed wrongdoers on the level of the Creator at the final judgment. Then the wrongdoers were very cursed to do injustice. Wrongful functions were

114

very cursed for the wrongful entities. Wrongful entities were very meaningful in the development of the system, because with the help from the wrongdoers were lots of shortcomings found. Due to lacks there were lots of problems, which became cursed often into the minds of humans concerning later times. In the minds of humans were so lots of cursed parts due to shortcomings. Due to the shortcomings, there were lots of cursed matters concerning the wrongdoers. Concerning the wrongdoers all the wrongdoers died at times into the shortcomings of the system. The shortcomings were due to the bad work of the Creator concerning the system.

In the system, there were shortcomings all in all quite a lot. All the wrongful entities were very cursing in regard to other wrongdoers, because the wrongdoers were very wrongful, because they were in the end children of the Creator so siblings to each other, which weren't allowed to have conflicts between each other. All the wrongdoers were very cursed due to their wrongdoing. The wrongdoers were very wrongful to other humans. Humans, to whom they were wrongful, might have been also righteous, to whom one shouldn't be allowed to be wrongful. All wrongdoers were very cursed due to the wrongdoing towards the righteous. The righteous rarely felt happy together with the wrongdoers, so the righteous usually avoided the wrongdoers once they observed them to be more wrongful. The wrongdoers had very wrongful agreements with the help from the appliance enchantments guiding the wrongdoers. All wrongdoers were very wrongful to all their directors as well.

The appliance enchantments which guided the wrongdoers were very cursed appliance enchantments due to the wrongdoers. However, the appliance enchantments still might have withstood the activities of the wrongdoers without becoming cursed. All the wrongdoers were cursed also due to the wrongdoers, because the appliance enchantments made the wrongful more wrongful with other wrongful. All appliance enchantments were very cursed towards the wrongdoers. All our wrongdoers were very wrongful to other wrongdoers. The wrongful had bad memories from earlier times in modern times. In modern times the wrongful entities were very cursed due to earlier times.

Earlier times were very cursed to all wrongful and the wrongdoers were hated in modern times. Beginning from modern times have the Creator's systems been destroyed from most of their part. Furthermore, on our planet Earth have the Creator's systems been destroyed in modern times. All the systems of the Creator are very cursing due to earlier times. When the Creator's systems were destroyed in modern times, the Creator became a super entity once again.

The Creator isn't allowed to be a super entity in difficult times, because during difficult times the super entities were destroyed due to injustice. All super entities are wrongful to a lesser extent, when the Creator's magics are stronger in them than in the more wrongful entities. The Creator's magics are a bit more cursing than the magics of other super entities. However, actually, the Creator is also the highest of all super entities, when he has from the super entities the greatest level of magic. All the Creator's magics are very cursed already beginning from earlier times. Very cursed magics are the closest to the Creator's magics, because the curse in magic comes forth due to wrongfulness in the experiencer of magic, so when the experiencer of magic is more wrongful than the magic itself, is the magic cursing.

All the eased magics are very wrongful magics, because they heal the mood of humans, which is wrongful mood magic. Making the mood better with eased magic is due to the lower energy consumption for the experiencer of the magic, when the mind gains more power from unused energy. Mood magics are very shining for entities, because they are more healing than the more wrongful magics, so magic improves the outlook, if the magic improves the mood. With good mood one becomes so better from one's outlook. Good mood magics are the level of the angels' own magic, so angels use mood magics. Mood magics are although wrongful magics, which can be exercised also in the world to improve the mood of entities. The mood of entities has a lot of meaning in the functions of entities. With better mood, entities are able to tolerate straining magics better and can use intelligence even in the most difficult situations. Real magics are very wrongful even as mood magics, because they affect into the destiny of entities with the help from other enti-

118

ties, which causes interference in the original order, because magic is cursing activity for thought functions.

Magics were better in earlier times than in modern times. This was due to that with magic one could do Creator's magic. All magics were very cursing to all our entities in earlier times, although, because usually magics led to the increase of injustice. Injustices increased with the systems of religion in modern times. With the systems of religion one has developed lots of magic as well to prevent the bewitching of the systems of religion with wrongful magic. Our systems of religion were very cursing originally, because our systems of religion were very fragile. Fragile systems are always possible to become cursed with wrongful magic. This cursing of the religious systems was very dangerous for the Creator, because if the systems start to become cursed the Creator has to do lots of repair work. Repair work was very cursing for the Creator already in earlier times, so the Creator did never want to do repair work, but he wanted rather to create new. All repair work was very cursing also. The Creator, therefore, created the systems of religion, so that with the systems of religion one could curse the superstition away in modern times. All superstition is very cursing for entities, because wrongful magics were very cursing for all entities.

All superstition did lots of evil in our earlier times. In our earlier times, all the wrongful were witches to some extent, which harmed with witchcraft other entities wrongfully. Magics did very bad result to all entities, which confronted it. So from witchcraft came very cursed activity. Cursed functions were very cursing to all the other entities. Entities were very wrongful often due to witchcraft. Witchcraft was so very harmful. All our magics were very cursing. With magic one was able bring about buildings and tools even for warfare. All playing with the tools created by the Creator were very cursed, because the tools created by the Creator added bumbling emotions. These kinds of emotions are wrongful according to the spiritual world. All wrongfulness is according to the spiritual world due to bumbling emotions. Entities want to bumble carelessly at times, into which sacrificial activity is based on, which is the most wrongful activity. All are wrongful finally, but wrongfulness is harmful activity most often. Usually the wrongful are very cursed from their wrongdoing, which is very wrongful. Activity without injustice is activity that is not cursed, which no other entity has done but one. This one is the Creator, when he is at his best.

At his best the Creator does only justice to his wrongful entities. The wrongful entities are very cursed from the Creator at times. Then entities are bitter towards the Creator's magics. The Creator's magics are very cursed magics, because no one can hold one's own against the Creator's magics. Almost no one has the Creator's magic in their use. All magics have ended for the Creator as well in later times, although they haven't, because the Creator can't become destroyed in any way. All the Creator's magics were very wrongfully placed into the use of the Creator concerning others, so that he would destroy his systems more with the help from those. The Creator's magic is such, that he could do injustice and pick wrongful things for himself. All injustices were wrongful activity of the Creator. The most wrongful magics were very cursing to all others except to the Creator. The Creator's magics were so very cursing to all the other entities at times, because he lived in very wrongful positions at times.

All the Creator's magics were abused by the entities of the Multiverse. All the abuse of magic was the activity of the entities of the Multiverse. The wrongful entities of the Multiverse were perfectly modified to the activities of the Multiverse. They were educated on a very high level with the functions of the spiritual world. All wrongful entities were victim entities of the Multiverse. Victim entities were so the activity of the entities of the Multiverse. To all their victim entities, the entities of the Multiverse were very wrongful. The activity of the victim entities was very cursed activity. According to the entities of the Multiverse, they had a permission to do injustice to their victim entities. All the entities of the Multiverse were very wrongful in this matter, because victim entities one shouldn't even have originally. All the wrongful magics were very cursing to others than victim entities as well. Victim entities are very wrongful activity according to the spiritual world, because no one should have victims, because no one deserves a so bad position in relation to others. The bad position is due to earlier times, when the entity which has gotten into bad position has done injustice to other entities and so deserved punishments. Such punishment activity is very normal activity that is in accordance with the spiritual world. All punishment activity is very wrongful when done to others by humans, because no one is justified to punish others. All punishment activity is very cursed activity. All cursed functions are cursed by the spiritual world beginning from earlier times. The most wrongful entities were very cursed due to their acts of injustice.

Cursing activity from the spiritual world is more acceptable than from other entities. The activity of the spiritual world is very wrongful activity, but the activity of the spiritual world is still holier that is more functioning than was even imagined. The functions of the spiritual world are rotated by the appliance enchantments, when appliances do all the cursed functions. All appliance enchantments do a lot of injustice to other entities, but they still have justice on their side. All appliance enchantments are very cursing to all entities to a lesser extent, because they function in the spiritual world, from where the universe is being rotated

in accordance with all the rules. All the rules
are very cursed measures, but they are better
than any other systems.